Farewell to the Starlight in Whiskey

Farewell to the Starlight in Whiskey

Poems by
BARTON SUTTER

AMERICAN POETS CONTINUUM SERIES, NO. 88

BOA Editions, Ltd. ❋ Rochester, NY ❋ 2004

First Edition

Publications by BOA Editions, Ltd.—
a not-for-profit corporation under section 501 (c) (3)
of the United States Internal Revenue Code—
are made possible with the assistance of grants from
the Literature Program of the New York State Council on the Arts;
the Literature Program of the National Endowment for the Arts;
the Sonia Raiziss Giop Charitable Foundation; the Lannan Foundation;
the Mary S. Mulligan Charitable Trust; the County of Monroe, NY;
the Rochester Area Community Foundation;
the Elizabeth F. Cheney Foundation; the Ames-Amzalak Memorial Trust
in memory of Henry Ames, Semon Amzalak and Dan Amzalak;
the CIRE Foundation,
as well as contributions from many individuals nationwide.

See Colophon on page 144 for special individual acknowledgments.

Cover Design: Ben Peterson
Cover Photograph: "The Back of Bart's Head" by Dexter Thue, courtesy of the
    photographer.
Interior Design and Composition: Richard Foerster
Manufacturing: United Graphics, Inc., Lithographers
BOA Logo: Mirko

Library of Congress Cataloging-in-Publication Data

Sutter, Barton, 1949–
  Farewell to the starlight in whiskey : poems / by Barton Sutter.— 1st ed.
    p. cm. — (American poets continuum series ; v. 88)
  ISBN 1–929918–57–7 (pbk. : alk. paper)
  I. Title. II. Series.

PS3569.U87F37 2004
811'.54—dc22

2004017341

NATIONAL
ENDOWMENT
FOR THE ARTS

BOA Editions, Ltd.
Thom Ward, Editor
David Oliveiri, Chair
A. Poulin, Jr., President & Founder (1938–1996)
260 East Avenue, Rochester, NY 14604
www.boaeditions.org

State of the Arts
NYSCA

Dorothea

Somehow your inexhaustible name
Contains all the other names I need.
It's an alphabet in itself,
A xylophone I play both loud and soft,
Both jamming with the band
And all alone, by myself, to myself.
Your name is yellow, red, and green.
Your name is both round and lean.
There's a doorway in it, and I see you
Standing there—black hair, white robe—
Waving me goodbye. Goodbye, Dorothea,
And hello, what's this? These consonants
And vowels have all the salt and savor of your skin!
Your name is deep and great as the greatest
Of all the Great Lakes, and I have set sail
Among its many syllables, I have drowned
In the unfathomable nonsense of your name.
Your name contains entire words—
Ah, the, O!—shimmering with meaning
And senseless as the sighs and groans
I utter when making love with you,
Dorothea. What a language!
It's all Greek to me, and Hebrew, too.
It's Indo-European and Chinese.
It's all Swahili and Icelandic, Dorothea,
And as Irish as you are. You are
What your parents named you, Gift of God,
And indeed you have saved me
From the drought of wordlessness,
The gnashing insomniac babble of my loneliness,
And therefore I have made a new religion
In your name, and I practice and pronounce it daily.
I adore thee, Dorothea. And therefore I proclaim
The delicious and exquisite language of your name.

Contents

I

II

III

IV

V

VI

I

My son, eat honey, for it is good,
and the drippings of the honeycomb
are sweet to your taste.

—Proverbs 24:13

Sweet Jesus

I found you, my lush, curvaceous savior,
Nailed to the old rugged cross of your life
As if cursed, caught, condemned to stay there.
Sweet Jesus with breasts and black hair,
I took you down, dressed your wounds,
Woke you from your midlife swoon,
And made you my unlawful wife.
You drank the gall of my despair
But swore there was another way.
Our bodies would be the wine and bread
On which we fed. We came alive there,
Nourished by grief, by tears and saliva.
And, lo, the stone of sorrow was rolled away;
Together, we rose from the dead.

The New Green

An overcast afternoon in mid-May.
The trunks of the aspens look silver today.
Tomorrow they might be olive or black,
But today they are silver. The leaves are lime-green,
As if lit from within. I love this new green,
So yellow and tender. I've loved it
Each year of my life, but never like now.
I'm driving north, my favorite direction,
But doubly so since it brought me to you.
The plum trees step out from the dark evergreens
And show off their blossoms. I love that fresh white.
I'm still too far south, but here in the car
I'm already there. Your daughters are sleeping.
We speak in hushed tones. I love your low voice.
The brandy is amber. Your eyes are light brown
And lit from within. You smile the smile
I survived all these years to discover. Oh, lover,
I love the crescent moon of your smile,
The curve of the road, the slope of your back,
The black of your hair, these black-and-blue rivers,
The buds of your breasts and the buds of these trees.
I'm very fond of the blonde and brown weeds,
But I love the love in your light brown eyes,
And now, more than ever, I love this new green.

Consider the lilies of the lake.
Unlike the lilies of the field,
They have never heard of Jesus,
They are ignorant of Easter, and yet
Each year they resurrect themselves
Out of themselves, out of water and sunlight.
They show the water and the sunlight what they are.
They do not have the shape of trumpets,
They do not blare their beauty,
They only open slowly, like so many women.
Rising from the waters, they bare themselves
And shine, suspended in the waters.
Aroused by the wind, their wet leaves lift,
And their undersides show red.

They are purposeless, these lilies,
Though beavers fatten on their roots,
And the bull moose wades in among them
Right up to his beard and eats.
He raises his huge head, he grunts and blows,
Water runs off his jaws. His antlers,
Spread like the wings of an eagle, are tangled
With flowers and greens.

The lilies of the lake do not exist for us. They simply are.
You seldom see them from the road. They grow
In silence, unobserved, in shallow bays of northern lakes,
Guarded by the swords of spruce and tamarack.
And that's where we are now, my love. The lake is blue,
The sun is warm, and the wind that riffles waterlilies
Also rouses us. It cools us and carries
The aroma of the forest that makes us both feel drunk.
This is exactly where we've always longed to be—
Here, among the lilies, unafraid of thunderheads

Massed on the horizon. We will reach the shore,
Make camp, eat, love, and sleep
Right through the storm. If lightning strikes us,
We will die, but this will make no difference.
The white-throated sparrow will still sing at dawn,
And the smallmouth bass will break the surface.

You turn and smile at me from the bow
And point where you would have us go.
I stroke a lazy J in the water to correct our course—
A little J for Jesus or The Joker or for Joy—and we enter
The garden of liquid delights. Or is it
The other way round, and you are in the stern,
I'm up front, and it's your smile rather than the sun
That warms my back? I only know
The lilies part for us, the garden opens.
The leaves of the lilies whisper, and their blossoms
Drown beneath the bottom of our boat.
We glide on through in our silver canoe,
And, when we pass, the lilies rise again.
When we pass, the lilies of the lake close again behind us—
Undisturbed, eternal, fragrant, and calm.

You think you're the queen of the Milky Way?
You think you're the mermaid in somebody's dream?
You, with your mouthful of metal molars?
You, with your outsized incisors?
You and your big mouth,
You and your wrinkled neck.
You, with the big brown mole on your leg
And the other one marring your back?
You, with your crabby fingers
And feet like cold fish?
You, with your goofy, wobbly boobs,
You saunter around with that absurd
Bird's nest between your legs
And think you're an angel on fire?
Think you're the wild witch of the woods?
Think you're the princess of darkness?
The mother of all my happiness?
Think you're the goddess who ate my heart?
Listen, lady. I made you up. Baby,
You ain't nothin' without my need.

The Boy Birch Tree

Lady of trees and flowers, you
Have planted a flowering tree in my name
And named me every tree and shrub
You started in your yard—working
From grief, fingers groping raw, cold earth,
Feeling your way toward some belief—
And walked me into the woods to find
The Balm of Gilead, uncurling its new leaves,
The source of that sweet perfume
Which has haunted us all of our lives.
But for all of your generous energy,
I have worried about your daughters—
How I could help you raise them,
What blight I might inflict, how they might
Choke my own new growth, and, worst,
The wild jealousy you generate in us all.
But one bright afternoon you brought
Your girls and flowers and food.
And there in my own backyard, you found
The boy birch tree. "Look," you laughed,
"He's shedding his skin like a snake.
I love when they do this." You peeled away
A shred of old, brown, loose, translucent skin
To show the bright white bark below.
"See?" you said, and we laughed.
A small, unadulterated happiness.
At last, before you drove away, I saw
The look on your daughter's face as she looked
At the look on mine as I returned your gaze,
And I felt the sort of faith you feel
When you set a plant in the dark, moist ground,
Imagining green though the grass is brown.

Sunday Morning

Daylight breaks on the flowering crab,
On the grass and the white garage.
Church bells shatter the silence.
And I have been broken, too.
My wife is gone. The house is bare.
I have lost friends, reputation,
What little money I had.
I walk the echoing halls of my house,
Singing your name to the tune
Of the Hallelujah Chorus.

Peregrine

In those days a decree went out
From the Stearns County Courthouse. I was free
To love you as I wanted, and I wanted you
With all my skin. That very weekend
We came together in a hotel room
Thirty stories high above the city
And saw how love was doubled
And redoubled in the floor-to-ceiling mirrors,
How our earthbound, mortal bodies
Came rushing forward from infinity
And exploded in that instant
When we shed our clothes and flew
Into each other's arms. There were mirrors
Everywhere in that high room
And out the window, too.
For when we rested from love's labor
And sat looking out, opposite,
Above the tallest building of the city,
We saw a peregrine
Sailing like a kite above the canyons.
As we watched the falcon flash and turn,
We hushed, and the flesh along our arms
Dimpled with excitement. And then the moment came.
Who knows how they know or how they have the gall to go?
Intuition must insist: *Do this now or die.*
The falcon folded his wings and dropped,
A living bomb, in his heart-stopping stoop,
One hundred eighty miles an hour headfirst toward the
    pavement.
And then the opening of wings, the swoop,
The rising up, and all that open sky.
He might have gone right on like a bullet,
But he turned, then, and alighted
On a cornice of that manmade sandstone cliff,

Where he was greeted by his mate. We gasped,
And a thousand empty windows gaped
As the peregrine, who knew his mate,
His fate, what he was for, cried kyrie
From his aerie in the bright blue air
High above the city.

Sunflowers

All my life long I was lonely
As the peat bogs of Beltrami County—
Depressions, dark water, a black spruce or two—
But then I saw you in that blazing yellow dress
And discovered the sin of covetousness.
How come you were another man's wife?
Why had I lived someone else's life?
How could Fate make such a monstrous mistake?

The first time I entered you,
You said, "Welcome home." I've carried you
Inside me ever since. The first time
You took me to your lonesome place
Up on Lake of the Woods, I stood
Gazing at the jack pines, the cattails in the creek,
Dazed, amazed, a traveler
Back from a disastrous expedition.

That night brush wolves howled round the house,
But you were warm and naked in my arms,
And since then I have witnessed
Many wonders in that cold, hard land:
How sandhill cranes float through fog,
How pelicans turn at the top of the sky,
How the sunflowers, somehow, seem to agree
And bow down by the thousands to the east.

Before Supper

Some day, Darling, we will be dirt,
Less alive than the weeds and green mush
Adrift in the bay out of which
We pulled that pike early this morning.
I cleaned him with a few quick cuts
And threw his guts in the woods.
Some day, Darling, we will be less than that,
But for now we are freer than trees,
And, unlike the deer we frightened today,
We have hands and laughter and language
To speak of the ether beneath our skin,
The fire in our groins, the liquor of love
In our thudding hearts. I bring you
The odor of mushrooms still wet from the woods,
And you have the scent of alfalfa, fresh cut.
Lie down with me here on the grass
Right now, before supper, before we sit down
To feed the tender white flesh of that fish
To our own. Lie down with me here
On this earth, that supports us for now,
To which, all too soon, we return.

Anniversary

There's a haze of hornets in the apple trees.
Hummingbirds pierce the plums.
Late August already. Already
The summer is done.

The hay is laid low. The flax is knocked flat.
The heat has gone out of the sun.
You've braided the tops of the onions
And gathered the vegetables in.

I think of the women I injured
Before I found the right one.
It's been a full year since I joined you,
Stunned by what I had done.

The summer is over already. Already
Autumn has come.
Your hair spreads like smoke on the pillow.
My heart thrums like a drum.

Nocturne

I ask you to play. Delighted, you turn
Oddly formal, insist I sit in the wingback chair,
Extinguish the overhead light, and switch on
The little brass lamp that brightens the big book of music.
You sit up straight at the great upright harp, which is black,
A block of intensified night, and you turn
To a nocturne by Chopin, the sad one.

You take me away. I am flying to Poland,
And now you are driving the sleigh
Deeper and deeper into the forest, over and over
The singing snow, the black sky burning
With bitter stars.

But no, I'm right here,
Watching you work at your loom,
Weaving a spread for our bed from the indigo
Light of late evening, the purple of midnight,
Shot through with threads of deep red.

But no, this is music. I see the notes
You are reading, the shorthand for Chopin's emotions
And ours. There are only a few in the treble clef,
The first bright stars above the horizon, while down below,
The dark, heavy notes dangle in clusters like purple grapes.
Your strong hands press and press out the juice
Which is music, silence distilled, and we drink.

The piano disturbs the dreams of your daughters,
Who come whispering down the stairs in their gowns
And settle beside us like ghosts who are haunted
By music so moody it sounds more like silence
Than sound, the silence inside us which holds
All we mean to say but cannot, which holds us here
Together for now, in this place where language leaves off.

This music says everything is so simple!
The keys are black and white.
This music says yes, we were born to suffer.
This music says thank you for all of those nights
Your father smiled into his drink instead of your eyes.
This music says thanks to my mother
For dying so slowly, with so many screams.
Thanks to that man who hit you and hit you.
Thanks to that woman who hurt me and hurt me.
This music forgives and says no, your desire
For love and the dream that you might deserve it
Was not a mistake. There were things you had to go through.

But now we have come to this clearing under the stars,
And you lift your hands off the keys. We climb
The stairs to sleep and wish the children good night
And wish each other good night, good night,
Stretch out naked and smooth, entwine, swoon,
And enter the music, leaving our bodies
Behind, though our bodies know they are safe
Until we return from that nocturnal space
Beyond joy and sorrow—deep, deep dream we deserve—
Whoever we are, wherever we go.

An Apple Branch

The trees were dripping rain that day,
   But then a gusty wind
Blew all the ragged clouds away
   And let the light break in.

You cracked wet branches off the crab
   With apples like bright bells.
You wore off-white, while I was drab.
   We'd walked through psychic hells

To reach this quiet, sunshot room,
   This terrifying hour
When we announced our joy and doom,
   Trembling like flowers.

We'd broken sacred vows before;
   There were no guarantees.
If we grew sore, afraid, or bored,
   Who'd see that we kept these?

And still we stood in silence there,
   Exchanged a pair of rings.
I loved your face and short, dark hair.
   I loved your everything.

Your girls stood up with us, and then
   We lit four candles bright.
I'd never seen a family blend.
   I prayed for help, for light.

We stuck those candles in soft sand
   Around a heart-shaped rock,
And as we stood there, holding hands,
   Our friends began to talk.

Jean said that sonnet by Shakespeare,
   "The marriage of true minds."
Some folks were snuffling with tears,
   But I was feeling fine.

Then Robert made the whole room laugh:
   "You two look good together."
The past was just a lot of chaff
   Blown off by windy weather.

My brother sang a poem by Burns,
   "O my Luve's like a red, red rose."
Sweet thought, but marriage vows are stern,
   And how they hold, God knows.

God knows, I would have winced and blanched
   If I'd forefelt the pain
Or seen beyond my half a hunch
   The trouble we had claimed.

We cleared out all the cards and gifts,
   The withered wildflowers,
And drove away to find out if
   The life we'd dreamed was ours.

It seemed that only death could stanch
   The music in my brain:
O my love's like an apple branch
   That glistens in the rain.

How the True Work of True Love Truly Begins

So here we are, dirty dishes
Stacked in the sink,
Shoes and toys stranded on the stairs,
Crumpled clothing strewn around the room.
Where are the blossoming plum trees now?
What good were all those roses I bought?
Your sobbing tirade sounds as black
As a November brook strangling on ice.
Since you insist on speaking Arabic or Inuit,
I lie here wrapped up in myself
Like a mummy in his bandages.
Oh, hell. Oh, who can help us now?
My father's ghost, perhaps,
Reciting some dumb ditty as he tries
To find the words for Sunday's sermon?
Or the spirit of your former husband, who
Haunts the basement, banging pipes,
Shuffling stacks of lumber?
How about your mother, sitting up,
Clipping coupons, carping
To my mother's corpse, which has a headache
And so lies stretched out on the couch?
My ex-wife dangles from a hook beside our bathrobes,
And I can hear your dad just down the hall,
Washing his hands of us and whistling.
Now the true work of true love truly begins.
The toothless moon looks in at us and grins.

Night Fishing, Lake Polly

I spoke to nobody all day long
But the wind, my canoe, and a family of otters
Who chattered and hissed like my own.
Now I stand here on granite
And cast a white spoon at black water.
The slippery fish keep to themselves,
But the moon is afloat like a white waterlily,
And stars glint like stones at the bottom.

I talk to myself, that invisible being
Who haunts me most when I think I'm alone,
And I catch myself calling me *you.*
"You should quit fishing now.
You should head for bed soon."
Out here in this solitude smelling of cedars,
I seem to be both me and you,
And we are my father, my mother,
My lover, my brother, that ghost of the woods
Who sings in my blood, urging courage
And uncommon sense: "Everything breathes,
Even rocks."

    I cast for the island
But come up with nothing more than a glimpse
Of something that shimmers, then glimmers and grows,
Unrolling over the trees, a dragon of light,
Chinese. I am fishing for nothing
And land it again and again, nothing less
Than the northern lights and the moon,
Which is both high and dry, wetter than water,
And frosting the leaves of the trees,
As I know we are, too, both
What we are and are not, as I am
Living proof of this truth,

Standing on rock but feeling like water,
Filled with reflections but coming up empty,
Wildly happy here on Lake Polly,
Not catching walleyes and missing my wife,
Whose name is not Polly.

A Circle of Rock

I've got this little island all to myself,
Except for the pair of broad-winged hawks
Who blessed my arrival by shouting out loud
That the dead birch tree was theirs.
Okay, I told them, okay, okay.
The mergansers are back, the black ducks,
The loons. They all come in pairs,
But I'm out here alone.

Everything pleases me here in this place:
My tent—that small, soft house of green—
The coffeepot blackened by orange and blue flames,
The thick-headed hatchet sunk in a stump.
It's a tidy camp, with simple demands.
The sky is so clear I've forgotten my name.

I've left you behind, dear woman,
Dark wife, with the worries of winter,
The list of spring chores, the yapping kids
With their childish greed, the canary,
The dog, and the garden seeds.
I imagine you're busy, angry, and sad,
But I've given my guilt to the wild breeze.

Still, all afternoon a herring gull flew
Past me and past me, bucking the wind,
With his bill full of sticks and mud and moss
For the nest he was building around his mate
On a circle of rock twelve feet across.
He came so close I could hear his wings
As he worked upwind again and again.
He made me ashamed. I hated to think
How often I've let loose a weary sigh
When you've asked me to please pick up the kids,

Go get the groceries, take out the trash.
Out here on the island, I'm free of all that.

Night falls. A thunderstorm crackles
And roars through the dark. The wind grows
Terrific and rips at the trees.
The flimsy tent jerks. It flutters and snaps.
When I crawl out at dawn,
The rock is bare, the nest is gone.
But the birds remain, facing the wind
Like weathervanes. I imagine
They mourn—bewildered, bereft—
But who can say what herring gulls feel?
Waves break around them like white-hot flames.

Windbound today, I'll spend one more night
Feeding the fire, watching the moon,
But, much as I love to make you fret,
I swear to you, wife, I'll head home soon.
And I won't forget those desolate birds—
Their cries the very voice of the sky—
Stunned by their loss, huddled in shock,
Ruined by the wind, but still a pair,
Standing there on their circle of rock.

Milk

The anxious agony of raising kids
Drains the life from parents, who must grow
From cradling to tug of war to slowly letting go
And learn to live with worry till they're dead.
When I fell in with you, I felt both joy and dread
Because you came with two small girls in tow.
I said, "I do." I'm glad I did, even though
I sometimes feel I married them instead.

It helps me to recall that gauzy, green meadow
Where we saw a tawny fawn duck under
The belly of its watchful, patient mother
And deliver two hard headbutts to the doe,
Doing what it took to get the milk to flow.

The Necklace

Ten tough years, and you are still
The one I want, despite your steel
Backbone, anxiety attacks, the lunatic hysteria
You carry in your blood like a dose of malaria.
I've heard you murmur odd thoughts about God
And sob as you shoveled a grave for your dog.
I've seen you drive tractor, drag a bush-hog,
And hunt for lady-slippers in a quaking bog.
You can build a wooden fence and glaze a window.
I'm glad to have a wife who threads her own minnow.
The other night as you fried fresh walleyes,
I was way too shy to do what I felt,
But I wanted to kiss that necklace of welts
Where you'd been bitten bloody by fierce black flies.

Yardwork

Moldering leaves have clogged the drain,
So I clean the gutters in a pouring rain,
Then carry the ladder to the weathered shed,
Hunch on a stump, and shake out a smoke.
Raindrops dingle on the old tin roof.
For the moment, at least, I'm weatherproof
And backed by quarters of birch and oak,
Rakes and spades slung overhead,
A hose on a hook, an axe at hand,
A leaning tower of old paint cans.
Iris glitters, the lawn is lush,
And the years go by in a blurry rush.
The girls drive now, reject their bikes.
When was it we gave away their trikes?
Their sandbox blooms, a flowerbed.
The saplings you planted climb sky-high
As our parents whimper, groan, and cry.
I'm sheltered here by years of work,
Your deep green dream and the pains you took,
Building this tender hedge against death:
Flowering hawthorn and bridal wreath,
Forget-me-nots, lilacs, baby's breath.

Rose Hips

Observing this year's plump rose hips,
I thought of ovaries and your plush lips,
How pods will break, surrender seed,
And you crack open, moist with need.
A hummingbird arrived just then
And probed the blossoms one by one.
Those last few blooms were all but done.
Let's go back to bed again.

II

He made my mouth like a sharp sword,
in the shadow of his hand he hid me;
he made me a polished arrow,
in his quiver he hid me away.

—Isaiah 49:2

You can have your Keats and Shelley,
Whose precious poems grow ripe and smelly
With references to Roman gods.
Reading them, I drowse and nod.
What's with these bloody Englishmen
Who wish that they were writing Latin?
Take Spenser, too, and William Yeats,
Grown men who labored to create
A land of ghosts and airy fairies,
For whom the real and ordinary
World was just not good enough.
And while you haul away that stuff,
I'll search the fat, official books
For those I love, the overlooked.
Give me Hopkins, Burns, and Smart,
Who drew their ink straight from the heart.
Hopkins, who loved God and weeds,
Felt ashamed of his deep needs,
Twisted syntax, jammed his grammar
Into an agonizing stammer
Of dumbfounded praise. And Kit
Smart wrote that poem I can't forget,
Electric lines about his cat.
Who'd look for ecstasy in that?
Burns could write a juicy hymn
From gazing at his lover's quim.
Priests and madmen, bumptious boys
Embarrass scholars with the noise
They raise in praise of sky and earth;
Editors decide they can't be worth
Much more than a few pages
In anthologies that show the stages
Of the long, slow march of poesy.
That's what *they* think. As for me

And my house, we just ignore
Those Greek-and-Latin English bores
Who creep along in dry blank verse
As sober-sided as a hearse.
Life's too short. And so we turn
To some old ballad that still burns.
I'd trade that creepy-crawly junk
For one good dose of Hopkins, sunk
In his spectacular despair
Or one sweet sonnet by John Clare.
I swear I'd give up all the rest
To watch him find that mouse's nest
He noticed balled up in the grass.
He says he "progged" it as he passed,
And everything's so sharp and clear
You want to stand and shout, "John Clare!
There's a fuckin' mouse in there!"

The Rusty Wheelbarrow

So much depends upon
A rusty wheelbarrow
Filled with pumpkins
Ripe and green
Beside the front steps—
Our daughters' happiness,
Hacking features
In the faceless heads;
The spiced insides
Of November pies;
Trays of salty, toasted seeds;
The legacy of the contractor
Who walked the plank,
Wheeling the wheelbarrow
Over the years;
The firm foundations
Of middle-class homes
Owned by people
We'll never meet;
The bank account
Of the contractor's daughter,
Who sold the wheelbarrow
For all of ten dollars;
The empty space in her garage
Where she can pile pumpkins now
From here to Halloween.

So much depends upon
Our battered wheelbarrow,
Spattered with paint
And a crust of concrete—
My wife's pretty back
(She hauled in the harvest);
My shoulders next spring,

When I'll move raw earth
Into beds and hills
For tomatoes and squash
And pumpkin seeds;
Not to mention the little
Electrical thrill
I felt when I walked home tonight
And saw the wheelbarrow
In the porch floodlight
And the shining pumpkins
Like salvaged suns.

Wordsworth!

Wordsworth! thou shouldst be living at this hour:
Personal computers have replaced the pen,
Plays have been upstaged by television,
And prolix poetry lacks the pizzazz, the power
To compete with boomboxes or any of our
Angry cars and waterbikes. We are selfish men,
Big boys in love with noise. Come back again
And fix us with a disapproving, dour
Stare; intone a few nostalgic verses
To clear the acrid, gray, polluted air;
And learn, old windbag, just how much we care.
You were a sentimental blabbermouth,
And you can eat our dust, exhaust, and curses.
What the hell were you jabbering about?

To the Author of "I Think Continually of Those Who Were Truly Great"

Here's to long, tall Stephen Spender,
Whose poems could send me on a bender,
A man who let himself get caught
Saying that he continually thought
Of those who were truly great. What rot.
Continually! Truly! Professors bought
That line, anthologized and taught it, even.
Jesus God. Sir Stuffy Stephen.
I met him once. He had dandruff.
I was afraid to be too rough
On the old boy, but I wanted to say,
"Sir? Sir Stephen? *By the way*,
And I know it's getting rather late,
But are you *still* thinking of those who were truly, really,
    honest-to-goodness great?"

To a Vindictive Editor

Thank you for your rude response,
Just what every writer wants,
Proof his words, distilled like gin,
Can brighten minds, however dim.
Your vicious message, meant to maim,
Electrified me, much the same
As if I'd won authentic fame.
Such pompous, lunatic nonsense
Almost serves as recompense
For days of effort at my desk,
Taking my sad self to task.
I've showed your letter off to friends
Who've hooted at your poison pen,
Astonished that my work—"third-rate"—
Could generate such caustic hate.
So thanks for the encouragement,
Though that's not what you thought you sent.
Forgive me for my public praise
You misremember through the haze
Of years, frustration, alcohol,
Your general loss of wherewithal.
Best wishes to your missing wife.
Blessings on your empty life.
May no one shoot you dirty looks,
Even though they've read your books.
May folks no longer turn away
As if your face had ruined their day.
Thanks again for all your help,
And best of luck with your bad health.

Not Sleeping at Bill Holm's House

In the corner of my narrow room,
There's a double-barreled shotgun,
Which will not go off in this poem.
Reclining on the bedclothes:
A small stuffed bear and pink flamingo,
Which I set aside. Turning back the spread,
I am greeted by red flannel sheets
Bearing a Frosty the Snowman motif.
This bed is too loud to sleep on, and I am
Too wired with coffee and wild ideas to dream
But settle in, anyhow, with a volume by Sandburg,
A poet far better than I had remembered,
Who talks of the tombs and the grass
And passengers rocketing into the dark
Toward strange destinations, like Omaha.
What could be stranger than Omaha?
I'm a passenger, myself, in this crooked old house
Full of books and the ghosts of hot arguments.
Where are we going? The clock says two,
And, out in the yard, a barred owl asks, Who?
Who are you? I answer that I am
A passenger on the Minneota Express,
Bound for points west—Canby and Mars.
I can hear, in the next compartment, my comrade,
My host, the polar bear of American literature,
Cough and hack and growl in his sleep,
Which I envy. I can't count sheep
Or the number of books in this house.
In the outer room, a harpsichord waits
As patiently as a horse-drawn cab
In a story of Sherlock Holmes.
Who done it? Who knocked me out?
And how did it get to be daylight
And Bill banging out hymns

On the downstairs piano, just now
That sweet Shaker tune
"Tis a Gift to be Simple"? Tis! Tis!
Tis also a gift to be complex and ornery,
With a house full of music,
Cigar smoke and whiskey,
And Icelandic sagas
Preserved by farmers
For nearly a thousand years.

This

in memoriam
Ted Hughes

This thistle is magnificent,
Rising out of the sandy plain
Like a knight from the Middle Ages.
Tall as a man, it barely sways
In the wind that flusters the cottonwood trees
And flattens the grass on all sides.

This is the boy who bristled
Whenever his mother came near,
Who sent her away to the south
The same night he slaughtered his father.
Woe to his brother, tears and woe.
His brother's name is forbidden.
His sister fled long ago.

The pagan king of emptiness,
This thistle lords it over
Goatsbeard, milkweed, the tender
Foolish flowers.
His virtue is courage, his vice is contempt.
His blades are edged with silver,
His spiky crown is stuck
With studs and purple gems.

Meaner than an ice pick,
This thistle stands on the sandy plain,
Glittering like shattered glass,
Glorious, barbaric.

Driving Kloefkorn to the Airport

Suddenly folks are afraid of the sky
And brown-skinned men with beards,
But not old Bill, who flew up here
Without so much as a Barlow knife
So those with ears could hear
The man recite a children's rhyme
About a frog, his own choice words
On watching his grandmother wash her hair,
A passage exhumed from the Old Testament
On pissing against a wall,
A great cloudburst of praise
For the scorched Nebraska plains,
Words that sing so sweet
You'd swear they must wear wings.

Now I drive the old guy with the good, round gut,
Glasses that glint like chips of ice,
A voice like wood-fired maple syrup
To our laughable international airport,
Where he shall be lifted up, transported,
A common state for the likes of him.

The scrap woods thin to stubble fields,
And a marsh hawk flaps like a wet dishrag
Over the hill and down the creek,
Gaining no more height than the Wrights'
Flimsy contraption at Kitty Hawk,
But flying, defying the downward drag, and eyeing
The mouse of fear that flees with a squeak.

October 2001

Inverse Letter to John Engman

Sincerely, I am still your friend,
Though I can't figure where to send
These missives that I haven't written.
Dead letters for dead men, my friend.
You scrammed, and no one seems to know
Which constellation you call home.

When the blood inside your brain burst
Through that vein, you pitched headfirst
Into your grimy clawfoot bathtub,
Where you choked on your own vomit.
No time to think, "Goddamn it! Now what?"
Glug, glug, glug, glug. One man in a tub.
You stood there on your silly head
And held your breath for hours, days,
Swelling up and turning red,
Until they found you all but dead
And hauled you, comatose, away.
Instead of a dazzled audience,
You got a ride in an ambulance—
One more miscalculation,
Like thinking poetry would mean salvation.

Your funeral was good, sad fun.
Your shaky parents seemed quite stunned
When everyone turned out—psych techs
From Fairview, where you'd worked
With crazy kids and nervous wrecks;
Drinking buddies; poets; jerks
Who fantasized they were your friends;
Several former writing students
Stupefied with grief; a blend
Of decent folks and freaks to send
You on your way. The body you had left

Lay stretched out in a metal box
While we sat still in shock, bereft,
And heard your closest friends give talks
About the stand-up comedy,
The high jinks, and blue poetry
With which you'd tried to save us all.
You were one screwed-up miracle.

Caroline said that she had seen you
In a dream. As if on stage or screen, you
Flew, suspended, swooping, swinging,
An angel wearing cardboard wings.
You were you, still whole, unhurt,
Complete with clogs and ratty shirt.
As if to cancel any doubt,
A cigarette burned in your mouth.
That brought you back to life again.
The perfect eulogy. Amen.

We put you in a cushioned hearse,
The limo treatment you had dreamed
You'd earn by writing wild verse
And publishing in magazines.
Your talent was a kind of curse.
What career choice could be worse
Than making wide-eyed poetry?
A recipe for poverty.
The cortege crawled, and when we paused,
I saw through stardust flakes of snow
A cheerful, waving Santa Claus.
The world was what you'd always known,
As odd as Alcatraz or Oz.
As we crept past the movie house,
The glittering marquee announced
A lovely, cruel coincidence
That made me suck in air and wince.
In your hometown the current show
Honored poetry with *Il Postino*.

Wouldn't you know, that movie centered
On the poet who'd brought us together
Close to last call that first night
When, sitting in the smoky light
Of Lyle's bar, I overheard you
Raving on about Neruda.
I didn't even think to think
But ordered up a round of drinks—
For me, a rash, audacious act—
And came around to where you sat,
A grinning, small, suspicious Buddha.
We were buddies, just like that.
For twenty years, we chewed the fat
Of friendship, gossip, raw ambition
To write poems, our secret mission.

You were my most disturbing critic,
Throwing poison darts that still stick:
"Jesus, you're like Richard Burton!
You feel your every fart's important."
Naturally I'd rather think
Of those rare times when you would blink
At something I had written, swear,
Run your hands back through your hair,
And praise me with a puzzled stare.
But mostly I remember laughter,
Crackpot theories of our craft:
"At least one joke in every line
And everything will turn out fine."

Looking back, I'm just amazed
The way we burned up nights and days
In single-minded work and talk
About the red-hot poems we sought.
We groaned and grumbled what a crock
It was that our advanced degrees
Hadn't earned us lives of ease.
We both were stuck in dead-end jobs
And cursed the undeserving slobs

In university positions.
Grant them tenure and promotion.
They're nothing next to your devotion
In those years we knew each other
As defiant, anxious, bitter brothers.

I see you in white shirt, blue jeans,
Weaving through an angry stream
Of traffic once the bars were locked.
Thirsty for more booze and talk,
You light a smoke, dillydally
Down the street and up my alley,
Plunge right in among the flowers.
You don't care jack about the hour
But wake me, scratching on my screen.
I wonder, "What the—?" Check the clock . . .
Up to your neck in hollyhocks,
You laugh and sway and sing my name.
And all this time that small blue vein
Is pulsing in your funny brain.

It hurts to relive history;
That's why you haven't heard from me.
My memories feel black-and-blue,
And, though I've tried to write to you
To let you know what's going on,
I just can't seem to get beyond
Those first two stupid words, Dear John.

III

They hatch adders' eggs,
  they weave the spider's web;
he who eats their eggs dies,
  and from one which is crushed
    a viper is hatched.
Their webs will not serve as clothing;
  men will not cover themselves
    with what they make.
Their works are works of iniquity
  and deeds of violence are in their hands.
Their feet run to evil,
  and they make haste to shed innocent blood;
their thoughts are thoughts of iniquity,
  desolation and destruction are in their highways.

—Isaiah 59:5–7

Back in the Woods with George W. Bush

I have pitched my green tent on this island
    Where the leaves are beginning to turn.
I have carefully filtered my water,
    Found plenty of dead limbs to burn.

Soon the leaves will be falling like leaflets
    That encourage the grass to disarm.
The trees will be frozen like fathers
    Who howl and hold out their arms.

The shadows of children in Baghdad
    Will be frozen to hospital walls
While many of us are out shopping,
    Fingering things at the mall.

I landed a nice mess of walleyes
    Last night in the milk of the moon.
I slit them clean up the belly,
    Filleted them right close to the bone.

One fish bore bite marks on his body;
    It's kill or be killed down below,
And don't expect help from the heavens,
    When ospreys may drop from the blue.

The shadows of children in Baghdad
    Will be seared to the hospital walls
When an earnest American pilot
    Wraps them up in a fiery shawl.

Last night I heard wolves by the river
    Like sirens or wails of grief
Strung out in the silence that followed,
    Though the ruckus they raised had been brief.

The yipping of young ones among them
    Testified to the strength of this troop.
They will tear the hides off outsiders,
    Though they're loving inside their own groups.

The shadows of children in Baghdad
    Will be welded to hospital walls
When a slightly misguided smart bomb
    Takes care of them once and for all.

From here I can see a dark vulture
    Tilt in the wind like a kite,
His pinions flashing with silver
    As he slowly descends from that height

To land on a shelf of raw granite,
    To flap his black wings and strut,
Nod his naked red head in the sunlight,
    And bury his beak in fish guts.

And the shadows of children in Baghdad
    Flicker on hospital walls
While bombers, like flies on the ceiling,
    Slowly, triumphantly crawl.

Dick Cheney's Heart

Where is Dick Cheney's heart?
Does it bulge like a bubo
Under his arm?
Does it hang like a goiter
Below his groin?
Where is Dick Cheney's heart?
Polls reveal that most of the nation
Desperately want to know the location
Of Dick Cheney's missing heart.
Is it hiding out
With JFK's brain?
Did the CIA
Leave it out in the rain?
Where is Dick Cheney's heart?
Is it floating somewhere
In a large vat of oil?
Is it kept on ice,
Though it's already spoiled
Like something moldy
You'd find wrapped in foil?
Where is Dick Cheney's heart?
We're worried about
Our vice president.
He had a bad heart,
But who knows where it went?
Is it hunkered down
In the cave of his colon?
Has it gone underground
With Osama bin Laden?
Where is Dick Cheney's heart?
Dozens of questions
Clamor for answers,
But this one would do for a start:
Where is Dick Cheney's heart?

A million citizens rally for peace,
And the TV reports that the president sneezed.
They have counted the droplets per cubic foot
Expelled from our leader's nose and throat;
They assure us he's stronger than any disease.

Angry grandmothers holler for peace,
But the anchor has more important news:
The president's dog has no fleas!
There follows a lengthy interview
With the animal's vet, who vows it's true.

Thousands of veterans march for peace,
And the network knows we'll all be pleased
By this rare footage from the president's ranch:
The commander-in-chief out hunting doves,
And here he is eating his lunch!

A man without legs protests the war,
A multitude responds with a roar,
But now this: The president loves
His wife! Laura, the Head Librarian,
No longer recalls why she married him,

But she's just reread *The Wizard of Oz*
And explains that we have to attack because
Her husband believes in the Baby Jesus,
And aren't we a Christian nation?
Reporters nod, taking dictation.

Nuns are singing no to war,
But the network provides interpreters
To read the satellite picture's blur.
Only buildings will be bombed in our name.
There will be no corpses, the anchor claims.

Women fasting in front of the White House
Can't keep the First Couple from going out.
The president waves his blessing and thanks,
Followed by photos of American tanks,
After which the screen goes blank.

The flag would like to relax,
To hang slack and satisfied
As a woman who's had some sweet sex.
But there's always another disturbance:
War, and rumors of war,
My governor can beat up your governor,
My president is prettier than your president,
Yeah, yer big fat mama wears combat boots.

And the flag is very sensitive;
It barely survived a violent childhood,
It can't help itself, it reacts
To the littlest thing.

So the flag wears itself out,
The stars start to fade from the blue,
As they do in the dawn
When we stay up all night with our worries.

So the red-and-white clown pants
Flap in the breeze, even though
The joke's over, come on, you guys,
Let me down.

The flag has no choice;
It hangs on, hangs on
Like a water-skier
Tied to a demented powerboat,
The pilot dead at the wheel.
The speed, the wind—
It was thrilling at first,
But now it's boring and scary both.
Aren't we there yet? Any idea
What country we're in?

The President's Prayer

Our Father who art in Washington,
However hollow Thy fame,
Thy thingdom come,
Our will be one
At home as in foreign nations.
Give us this day our deficit,
And forgive us our bombing passes
As we bomb those who might surpass us.
Lead us not into conservation,
But deliver us from free will.
For ours is the thralldom,
The war, and the gory.
No matter, whatever,
Your man.

Jail Time

As our bombs were blowing up Baghdad,
   I was jailed with Rodney Moose
And eight more men who'd had it
   With the deadly daily news.

When letters and furious phone calls
   Fail to stop your leaders' lies
And candlelight vigils prove futile,
   Is there anything left to try?

We locked up the Federal Building
   And sat tight, two to a door,
The cautiously law-abiding
   Next to those who'd been reckless before.

We sat in the cold for two hours
   While gunmen debated our fate.
Some people brought us flowers,
   Though others were irate.

When the cops arrived with the wagon,
   We each had a chance to speak.
Did we want to walk or be dragged in?
   Their leather jackets creaked.

They cuffed our wrists in plastic
   And patted our bodies down,
As if a weapon more drastic
   Than a pencil might be found.

The wagon circled the building,
   Collecting a pair at each door.
We offered each other shy greetings.
   The port-a-prison grew warm.

A double reverse Houdini,
  Peter unzipped my coat,
Returning the hand he had slipped free
  Back in its plastic knot.

In jail they took our shoelaces
  And confiscated our belts
As if they needed to save us
  From strangling ourselves.

They took away our identities,
  But we still knew who we were:
A birdwatcher in his seventies,
  Recalcitrant Catholic workers,

An atheist, two preachers,
  An Ojibway man named Moose,
A poet, a clubfoot, a teenager
  Were among the unconfused.

Till they took our prints, we languished,
  Chatting or trying to snooze.
The guards took a special relish
  In calling out, "Mr. Moose?"

They shot him with their camera.
  Then Rodney, who'd lost a finger,
Smiled and held his hand up
  To say he'd save them ink.

We met a man who'd been hauled in
  To stay for thirty days,
Though the reason seemed appalling:
  He'd skipped out on AA.

A war, undeclared by Congress,
  Dismembered kids that day.
Our group was charged with trespass
  While the president went his way.

Consoling ourselves with stories,
    We chortled at Scott's report:
How he'd linked a favorite rosary
    Through the handle of his door

And the job turned suddenly scary
    For the cop who cut the locks;
When he squeezed, it wasn't the rosary
    But the bolt-cutter that broke.

We laughed and decided on tactics
    Even more frightening:
The next time we took action
    We'd agree on a hymn and sing.

No one likes being restricted,
    But our day in jail was short.
They sent us home with our tickets;
    We'd meet again in court.

There's a comradeship among people
    Who pay for what they do,
So we said, though our efforts seemed futile,
"Nice getting busted with you."

Captain Rummy, Henny Penny, Hammurabi

"I read eight headlines that talked about chaos,
violence, unrest. And it just was Henny Penny!—
'The sky is falling.' I've never seen anything like it!"

—Secretary of Defense Donald
Rumsfeld

Iraq's museums had been looted, and you whined
  How Chicken Little journalists were failing
To appreciate the freedom war had won.
  Annoyed, you said they said the sky was falling.

Was it news to you that many found your views
  Appalling? For days, the heavens had been falling,
Raining ragged steel and phosphorescent fire to subdue
  A people who, regardless, kept on crawling

From the wreckage of their restaurants and homes.
  You'd sent your tanks to guard the Oil Ministry
But couldn't understand why anyone would moan
  About ten thousand years of human history

Or why the pliant media had turned
  Against you just because some Ali Babas
Had run off with artifacts of Babylon and Ur
  Or stolen tablets that contained the Code of Hammurabi.

Freedom, you explained, was naturally untidy.
  As for looting, arson, automatic weapons,
Ransacked hospitals, loose rounds of RPGs,
  You said, with eloquence, "Stuff happens!"

Perhaps your early training as a pilot
  Inculcated this distant God's-eye view

In which a wedding party turns into a target
　　For cautious, polished bureaucrats to rue.

But now your supersonic flight is stalling.
　　Eject, and softly parachute to earth
To see how parents learn the sky is falling
　　And tell us what you think your family's worth.

Your men shot up the Kassims' family car
　　And killed three of their children by mistake.
We know. Stuff happens. Accidents occur.
　　Thank God an Army hospital could take

Both broken parents and their wounded daughter.
　　Provided with a bed for two long nights,
The five-year-old, her mother, and her father
　　Were displaced by soldiers hurt in firefights.

Left blanketless beneath the freezing sky,
　　The girl complained, "I'm cold. I'm getting colder."
What could they do, her mother asked, but listen as she died?
　　"My arms were broken, I could not lift or hold her."

This story may not move you, Donald Rumsfeld,
　　But sin-sick soldiers will not follow you
Because you've grown too deadly numb to feel,
　　And soon, Flyboy, the earth will swallow you.

The Neocon Con

Although they'd mostly missed their war,
The neocons had plans in store.

The cocky thoughts of William Kristol
Called for rosary and missal.

Woolsey said get ready for
Nothing less than World War IV.

Defense investors round the world
Bought the words of Richard Perle.

Profundities of Wolfowitz
Ensured that kids were blown to bits.

All these men could count on Cheney
For intelligence chicanery.

How many American soldiers died
Defending Donald Rumsfeld's pride?

Let widows mail their funeral wreaths
And folded flags to Douglas Feith.

Selected president, their moron
Brayed this motto, "Bring 'em on!"

We may forget dead soldiers' names
But not the neocon con game.

IV

Even in laughter the heart is sad,
and the end of joy is grief.

—Proverbs 14:13

Somewhere along in your forties,
You realize a lot of people are dead,
But not you. Not yet.
Driving past the hospital, you recall
That curly-haired medical student,
Her quick hands, her eager mouth.
She had a sweet apartment above the park,
Fragrant with eucalyptus. Remember
Those silly games you played
With her silver stethoscope? She lost
Both breasts, those breasts you used to kiss.
She's gone. And you can't believe you can't
Visit your pal, the poet,
Whose tiny apartment was jammed
With books, laundry, beer cans,
Ash trays big as hub caps.
You'd clear a space and smoke
And smoke and laugh and laugh.
That room smelled bad
But also good. He's gone,
Beneath the snow, beneath the earth.
You drive by your grandmother's place.
When she opened the door, she'd shout your name
As if she'd won the lottery, then add,
Immediately, "You want something to eat?"
She had stubble on her chin
And a glint in her eye
As she shared a juicy story
She'd been keeping warm for weeks.
She wore too much perfume,
But it couldn't cut the odor
Of coffee in that room.
Perhaps you don't miss these people
As much as you miss their apartments,

Those little chatterboxes,
Those friendly, small efficiencies.
You imagine two men making love
In that quiet place above the park,
An old woman stroking her cat
In the poet's rank apartment,
A retarded man struggling
To open a can of tuna in that room
Where your grandmother laughed
Over photographs of her youth.
How sad, you think. How strange.
Then the car behind you honks,
And you see that the light has changed.

Mrs. Winters

When I was a boy and my mother came apart
From leukemia and chemo and the surgeon's knife,
I jumped on my bike and pumped three miles
Up the winding river road through the blinding yellow light
To the small, kempt farm of Boyd and Evie Winters.

> I loved my mother, but she couldn't love me.
> She was crazy with drugs and agony.

Boyd, a sturdy man, was frequently gone
Driving his cattle truck over-the-road.
They had two sons. Roger was a pudge
But shared his go-kart. Kendall squawked,
Flopping in his wheelchair, drooling
With pleasure at his mother's touch.
I didn't bike that far for *them*;
I went for Mrs. Winters. Evelyn.

> I loved my mother, but she couldn't love me.
> She was bald as a doll, and her sick breath reeked.

Leggy and blonde, a palamino gal,
Evie had a voice that made me melt.
Her patience with her palsied son,
Crooning soft and stroking him, stiffened me
With jealousy. She told me calmly
Of the calf in the barn, the cow and the bull,
Passing on the rudiments shamelessly.

> I loved my mother, but she couldn't love me.
> Twisted in the sheets, she couldn't even see.

Evie took some time for me. We walked
The green grove, watching for warblers—

Redstarts and yellows, the black-throated green—
And smiled at their zigzag, zany songs.
Mrs. Winters watched the birds, and I watched her,
Her soft breasts bulging the white of her blouse.

      I loved my mother, but she couldn't love me.
      She was screaming for Jesus and more morphine.

Milk and cookies and the slow ride home.
I was pedaling through Eden, though I didn't know it then,
Despite the blue heron, white egrets in the trees.
Halfway home, I stopped, frozen in the sun,
Gazing at the river, the blurred horizon,
Knowing I was guilty of an awful sin.

      My mother loved me, but I'd chosen another.
      Twelve years old, I loved a grown man's wife.
      I have kept and cherished her all of my life.

Dementia

My father has lost his mind.
There's next to nothing left to find,
But he wanders the house anyway,
Hunting for it night and day.

He shuffles along with baby-steps.
Drool runs off his lower lip.
He stands before the full-length mirror,
Entranced by the ghost of himself in there.

My father has lost his grip.
He has to lower his head to sip
His coffee. He moans for his wife
To help him operate his fork and knife.

He hasn't lost his appetite,
But watching him eat is a shameful sight.
He can't be trusted to find the pot
And soils his diaper more often than not.

He used to like to hike and swim,
But this is what's become of him:
He picks the litter off the floor.
He tries the lock on every door.

He drums the chair, he beats his thighs.
He gives out little groans and sighs.
Smiling, he stands and claps his hands.
He fiddles with his wedding band.

He descends the stairs; he climbs the stairs.
Whatever he wanted wasn't there.
Never a man to make a fuss,
He hides in the shadows and grins at us.

The man was a preacher, years ago,
But now he's down to "yes" and "no."
He cheered for me at football games.
Now he can't recall my name.

Because I used to look up to him,
I rub his back and hum a hymn.
His back is hunched. He's got a limp.
He looks like a little, old, gray-haired chimp.

He drifts through the rooms called night and day.
What was it he wanted, anyway?
There's next to nothing left to find.
My father has lost his mind.

Busy, distracted, I answer, "Hello?"
And a husky, hurried voice murmurs,
"I made an appointment to have an abortion today?"

The moment of silence that follows
Expands, turns inside out
And back again. I know
This woman has made a mistake, but think
Maybe not, given how, still,
Half a century on, a part of my brain
Remains plain dog, a setter on point,
An eager springer who leaps for a look,
A hungry hound who sniffs and howls,
Who wants it, wants it, just that, slick slit,
No forethought, no knowledge, no consequence.

Does she think I'm her husband, her father,
Her lover, her doctor, or what? Is she
Calling the clinic to cancel, is she
Going to be late, did she maybe miscarry?

All of this goes through my head
Without words in a wink,
And I want to say, "Sweetheart, oh, honey,
You have to be careful whoever
However whenever you fuck,"
As if she didn't know that now
And all my thoughts weren't useless
Yapping. Bark. Bow-wow.

Impotent, flustered, what can I do
But say, "Sorry.
You've got the wrong number."
And read the digits off my phone.

She moans, "Oh, I'm sorry."

Father, husband, lover, brother,
I'm a stranger stuck for words
Except, "I'm sorry, too. Good luck."

First wife, lost friend, sad ghost,
My long amnesia lifts at last,
And guess what memory haunts me most.
More than fifteen years have passed

Since we caught the bus to Ullapool
But failed to ditch the damned tourists
Who swarmed like minnows in a school.
We'd crossed an ocean to come to this?

Mobs of Americans everywhere.
I sulked in a corner of our B & B,
Numb with anger, cold despair,
Knocking back the gold whiskey.

You coaxed me out to take a meal,
Where we met a boy from Aberdeen
Just back from hiking in the hills.
Shy but warm, windburned and lean,

He looked so much like our dead friend,
The one you'd once betrayed me with,
We didn't want the talk to end.
He told us we'd been tricked by myth

But sympathized and laughed a lot.
"The Highlands crawl with nice tourists
Who'd like to meet authentic Scots.
The trouble is, we don't exist."

That night we found a loud Ceilidh
And met a singer my brother knew
Whose northern hospitality
Included a room and brown home-brew.

Why didn't I dance with you that night?
I ordered one more glass of booze,
Stiff, as usual, too uptight,
And focused on those boots and shoes

That thumped so hard they had me asking
How the floor could bear the load.
They finished with that wild anthem:
You take the high road, and I'll take the low road . . .

And I recall Scotland without you.
We won't be bending over pics
To reminisce. Like me, no doubt, you
Try to forget what can't be fixed.

Remember, though, how we drove that night
To the singer's village of Rosehall,
And how, in the mist, our bright headlights
Caught the flight of a short-eared owl?

And then another and another,
Rising off the steaming road,
Two dozen, maybe, altogether.
Each time, of course, the driver slowed,

And time did, too, till we were back
In a supernatural Scottish ballad,
Flush with omens, knights who hack
Through steel and mail to bone and blood.

We hoped our driver wasn't lost.
Each owl gave our nerves a thrill,
Fluttered like a great, soft moth,
And left us happy, hushed, and chilled.

We wandered Europe hand in hand,
Less like lovers than two friends
Who couldn't start to understand
How the fairy tale would end.

Back home, we learned to curse and howl
And found an ocean we could not cross.
These days, when I recall those owls,
They rise as ghosts of all we lost.

Block Party

"I saw three bodies covered with sheets
Stretched out on the lawn at dawn,
And all I could think was, 'What
On earth will the neighbors think?'"
Greta laughs and shakes her silver hair.
She's short and plush and lovely still,
Though she's into her seventies now. She turns
Her grin on Jim, her son, who's home
Here in August to visit the folks,
Who pulled this boyhood magic trick,
Escaping the suffocating house
To sprawl in the cool and soothing grass,
Pulling his children along. Greta
Tells him our names in vain, falls back
On those of neighborhood ghosts
Who owned our houses long ago.

It's hot, way hot for here, the sun
So hard we retreat into softening shade.
Greta's Frank goes all the way back
To '36 to remember heat so strong.
Potato salad is heaped in hills, patties
Are waiting on plates, but nobody lights the grill.
We slug down soda and beer, mutter and chat.
Then Greta disturbs the peace: "They found
A big tumor on Frank's spine." A sigh
Goes up like smoke, followed by wounded sounds:
"Don't tell me." "Oh, no." "If there's anything . . ."
There's nothing the doctors can do
But shrink the tumor to ease the pain.

And now we see what we missed before:
How Frank has faded, paper-pale,
Frail as an Arctic flower. Soldier,

Teacher, father, coach, gardener
Going, going, gone. And Greta,
Bound to go on alone,
Too Midwestern to sob or wail,
Embodies our regional motto: *Let's
Don't Make a Fuss*. Her gaze is strong
As a star, giving off light that enters us
As she says, with a trembling smile,
"And so . . . so here we are."

Stress Echo

They shave me, oil me, wire me up.
I exercise to wind myself,
Lie on my side while the whitecoat runs
A kind of ball bearing over my chest,
Then stops his hand: Behold, my heart
Breaks into view on the silver screen!
Is this my old friend, the seat and seed
Of so many emotions, squeezebox of dreams
And aspirations, love thumper, sump pump,
Living bellows that swells with blood,
That thrills to music, ta-dum, ta-dum,
And drums whenever I walk or run?

It hurt last week, but I know what's wrong:
Work and worry, not enough fun.
And now I remember biology class,
How we cut the miniature heart from a frog;
It went on pulsing in a Petri dish
Long after the lank green corpse lay still.
But this one is large as a human fist,
Squeezing, relaxing, clenching, and easing,
Milking my blood through miles of veins.
Strong and slick as a rainbow trout,
It's holding steady in the rushing stream
While I wheeze and gasp like a fish on the bank.

What pity I feel for that little valve
Going tick, tick, tick—my tireless,
Throbbing pocket watch, that
Indefatigable, tiny worker,
Taken for granted too long. High time
I said thanks to this dab of flesh
And my ancestors in the old country,
Digging turnips and raking thin hay,

Packing their trunks to sail away.
I see my dad's mother wringing out clothes,
Every last nail her husband drove,
My mom's old man holding the gun
To pound hot rivets in plates of steel.
His wife, who worked for the woolen mills,
Also hiked miles to country school,
Blew sparks alive in the iron stove.
Thanks to my mom for scrubbing the floors,
For canning green beans in clouds of steam,
For bucking in labor until I was born,
Postpartum depression, tender breasts.
While my heart still beats, forget me not
The miles my father walked in the war,
Living off rations, adrenaline fear,
Raggedy breath, and trembling prayer.

The heart is an organ for pumping blood.
Our efforts are carried away in the flood,
Mostly forgotten, misunderstood,
But we labor together for evil or good.
The dew on the hills is our element,
But, fish in the stream, we are ignorant.
The homes we own we really rent.
We speak a language we didn't invent.
The air we breathe was made by trees,
Grass, bindweed, bloodroot, heart's-ease.
And where is the justice we've done wrong for,
The peace and contentment we all long for?

Love muscle, clenched glove, triphammer heart,
Help me to tell my needs from greed.
Spitting image of the mercy seed,
Don't quit on me now. Suck it up. Jump-start.
The labor of others is our lifeblood,
And arrogance is for dunderheads.
The trucker, the trash man, the nightshift nurse
Have all put money in this bloody purse.
Workers unite in this hymn to my heart

And everyone else's counterpart,
Whatever breathes on the living spark,
Hard work going on and on in the dark.

V

The beginning of wisdom is this:
  Get wisdom,
  and whatever you get, get insight.

—Proverbs 4:7

Sober Song

Farewell to the starlight in whiskey,
So long to the sunshine in beer.
The booze made me cocky and frisky
But worried the man in the mirror.

Good night to the moonlight in brandy,
Adieu to the warmth of the wine.
I think I can finally stand me
Without a glass or a stein.

Bye-bye to the balm in the vodka,
Ta-ta to the menthol in gin.
I'm trying to do what I ought to,
Rejecting that snake medicine.

I won't miss the blackouts and vomit,
The accidents and regret.
If I can stay off the rotgut,
There might be a chance for me yet.

So so long to God in a bottle,
To the lies of rum and vermouth.
Let me slake my thirst with water
And the sweet, transparent truth.

At Quaker Meeting

We listen to the pigeons on the rooftop coo.
They're not your classic doves, but they will do.
The meeting house is musty, dim, and warm.
A girl unzips her coat. An elder folds his arms.
The silence deepens till we hear small rustlings,
Swallowing, slow breathing, someone's stomach rumbling.
Where is the peace that passeth understanding?
We breathe, stock-still, like cattle standing
At the feed bunks in the faint but rosy light,
Who don't complain or preach but simply stand and wait
For one who always comes, although he's sometimes late,
Hoping to be touched on heavy brow or shoulder blade
By him who breaks the ice so they can guzzle water,
Who dumps and spreads the mounds of sweet and fragrant
      fodder.

The Old Corral

The barn looks like a drawing, delicate and silver,
Pocked with holes where the bats and birds
Come and go as they please.
The spindly rails of the old corral,
Saddled with lichens, green and gray,
Are gradually giving way.
The heavy gate has fallen.
So many things I failed to control.
I rest my hand on the rusty pump,
The handle curved like the head of a horse,
And watch wind race through the waist-high grass.

Icebreaker

I saw *The Sundew*
Returning to port,
The crew dressed in snowsuits,
Helmets, and gloves
And fancied I'd like to work out there
On the dark, wild water,
In the cold, blue air.

Their work is no dream.
It's jarring and hard.
Their boat's called a cutter,
So you'd think it could slice,
But *The Sundew* breaks through,
As the rest of us do,
By butting and sliding,
Ramming and crashing,
Riding up on and smashing
The rock-solid ice.

The Thousand-foot Ore Boat

To live until we die—
The job seems just impossible.
The great weight of the past
Pushing us forward, the long future
Thrust out before us, and so little room to either side!
The least we can do is stay sober,
Look sharp. The thousand-foot ore boat
Slides through the ship canal
And eases beneath the bridge,
All engines thrumming,
Including the pilot's heart.

Handyman

The morning brought such a lashing rain
I decided I might as well stay inside
And tackle those jobs that had multiplied
Like an old man's minor aches and pains.
I found a screw for the strikerplate,
Tightened the handle on the bathroom door,
Cleared the drain in the basement floor,
And straightened the hinge for the backyard gate.
Each task had been a nagging distraction,
An itch in the mind, a dangling thread;
Knocking a tiny brass brad on the head,
I felt an insane sense of satisfaction.
Then I heard a great crash in the yard.
The maple had fallen and smashed our car.

Cocklebur

Tossing trash branches down the ravine,
Avoiding their whiplash, cutting and mean,
I stooped way too low and tangled my hair
On a stickery, plump, fresh cocklebur.
My wife was amused and tore the bur out
While I bowed my head and swallowed a shout.
That little land urchin, that green porcupine
Had been waiting to snag a warm body like mine.
The plant meant no harm; it just had a need
For something with legs to carry its seed,
But I learned a lesson from nature's tomfoolery,
That nasty piece of vegetable jewelry.
I could sympathize with the mangiest cur,
Having got caught by my own patch of fur.

Topsy-turvy Bird

This energetic little guy,
Who wears a dark line through his eye,
Blue-black back, and rusty breast,
Hardly ever stops to rest
But climbs our trees the wrong way round,
His worldview clearly upside down,
As if he thought the sky were ground,
Probing corrugated bark
For bugs and seeds from dawn to dark,
And, having worked his shift, plus overtime,
He's too worn down to sing or whine,
"What a way to make a living!"
He rests his weary feet and wings,
Relaxing in a hollow bole,
A resin-fragrant, downy hole,
Rightside up so blood will drain
Like hope and worry from his brain
To tingle in his twitching tail.
Do you suppose he thinks he's failed
Or stays up late to calculate
The itsy tidbits that he ate
Or somehow counts what he is worth
Or dreams of mansions in the earth?

Whistle Dance

My grandmother from Hinckley told
My brother and me, when she'd grown old,
How they used to dance in farm country
Way back in the twentieth century.
"We'd go down through the woods with kerosene lanterns
To Andersons' barn, where we held our dances.
The way that light flashed off the birches,
Why, it was like candles in those Catholic churches.
The girls wore shawls, but we soon got warm.
Just a big bare room, and nothing more.
What did we care? We stomped up a storm.
Tom had a sweet harmonica. Or a fiddle played
Far into the night. We stayed and stayed.
Sometimes we didn't have anything!
We'd hold our darn dance anyway,
If all we could do was whistle and sing."

October Soccer

for Bettina

The sweet days of summer are over and done,
But the girls are bronzed and beautifully fit.
Does anyone care who lost, who won?

The quick, brown girls still kick and run,
Though applause from the stands is muffled by mitts.
The warm days of summer are over and done.

Is the score 2 to 1? Are we still having fun?
The subs run in place, shiver, and spit,
Too numb to care who lost, who won.

The sweeper goes down and lies half-stunned,
Gets to her feet, shakes off the hit.
The soft days of summer are over and done.

When these girls give birth to daughters and sons,
Will they pass along this hustle and grit?
Will anyone care who lost, who won?

The earth is a ball, and so is the sun
That sinks as snowflakes begin to flit.
The sweet days of summer are over and done.
Does anyone care who lost, who won?

Fall Flowers

Sunflowers, primrose, butter-and-eggs,
These are the last of the gold.
Asters announce the annual disaster:
Our part of the planet turns cold.

Will we think of the snowflakes as flowers
So wild they'll never be sold?
Or will we grow dark and bitter
And wither before we are old?

Snow

When we buried my mother, years ago,
The weather was downright nasty.
At my father's grave, a bitter blow
Had us chattering and gasping.
Still, I love these little puffs of snow
Poised on the pearly everlasting.

VI

And they went away in a boat
to a lonely place by themselves.

—Mark 6:32

Love becomes duty and gradually blinds you,
Strangles, mangles, damn near defines you.

Your spouse no longer seems to find you
Electromagnetic. The kids won't mind you.

      Swing and pull. Put it behind you.
      Head on out where no one can find you.

Break the tendrils, vines that bind you,
The lockstep life that grips and grinds you.

Slide away on the silky water;
Bob and glide like a river otter.

      Swing and pull. Put it behind you.
      Round the bend. They'll never find you.

So your colleagues undermine you.
There's nobody here for you to whine to.

Your mind still roars like a motorcycle?
Watch that eagle slowly circle.

      Swing and pull. Put it behind you.
      Wind and sun will realign you.

Is this your life, this quick vacation?
Pass through the burn, note the devastation,

But see how the black seems almost designed to
Come back green? Well, you're assigned to

Swing and pull. Put it behind you.
A drink from the river might revive you.

Is there some secret you've been blind to?
Tracks in the sand may well remind you

Of a desperate message in dots and dashes.
Downstream, a rainbow leaps and splashes.

Swing and pull. Put it behind you.
Let the scent of cedar find you.

Here's a deer come down to drink.
Is there someone you should thank?

Someone you've been less than kind to?
Shuck the jacket that confines you.

Swing and pull. Swing and pull.
The river flows, but it's still full.

The river shines, black as lacquer.
What is it you've always hankered after?

Although you've only half a mind to,
There's still a chance that you might find you.

Swing and pull. Swing and pull.
Isn't this river beautiful?

Jack Pine

Oh, Jack Pine, I love you,
Even though you are dead,
Even though and even because
You aren't my kind and can't love me back.
God knows I've felt the same pointless affection
For women I've only gazed at across a room, to whom
I was never properly introduced
But went on loving wildly forever nevertheless.
Besides, I don't care what people call me
Anymore since anytime now, very soon,
I'll be a mumbling, daft, old man
Like my father before me,
And then I'll be dead,
Like my father before me,
So I might as well declare myself
Right here, clearly, while I can.

Jack Pine, I love you because
Your branches bend gracefully down toward the ground
Like the arms of a ballerina
In a certain modest position I can't name
But recognize at a glance, anywhere, even here,
Hundreds of miles from the nearest dance theatre.
Such poise. Such patient power. Brava! Bravissima!

Oh, I could say your drooping limbs
Resemble the down-curved wings of a bird
Protecting her brood, except you can't fly,
No matter how big the wind,
So that can't be right.

No, I see
I was more right before:
You're a woman, old woman, Jack Pine,

For your bare arms are bent,
Your skin has grown scales,
And you wear your tangle of twigs
Like a shawl of gray lace. Still,
Come sunset, your grace, you grow
Young once again, so dark and romantic I know
Your true name isn't Jack Pine, Jack Pine,
But must be Jacqueline.

Oh, Jacqueline,
Your silhouette is so naked,
So black and attractive against the afterglow
I can see clear through you to your future.
All your life long you have stood here
Patiently, rooted in rock, gripping
Your pairs of pine cones like little bells
That trembled in the wind and shook out
Their silent music for years on end.
For years on end you have swayed here,
Dancing in place, stretching higher, higher,
Straining after something you knew not what
But felt in your very xylem and phloem
Would be your fulfillment—something
Like the sky, like the sun, something hot—
You knew not just what but felt
An overpowering desire to be opened,
To be ruined, to be burnt black as dirt
By the all-consuming passion of him
Who would take you like a hero. I am not he.
I am only he who sings this hymn
In praise of you and tells you truly he will come
And ravish you, destroy you,
Releasing you at last
That your progeny might live. I am no liar.
He will surely come. His name is Forest Fire.

Blowdown

The needles of this white pine
   Have turned from green to red,
As if a tree should be embarrassed
   For falling on its head.

It never stood especially tall
   But had a certain grace.
It crowned this little island
   And now has left a space.

I paddle round the granite slab
   To view the underside,
The root system that let the pine
   Shine and grow upright.

Here's the lowdown. Here's the dirt—
   Shocking, crude, and raw—
Roots like writhing snakes, like hands
   That, reaching, grasp and claw

To get those nutrients they need.
   They groped both night and day—
Thirsty, greedy from the seed—
   And still clutch clots of clay,

Lumps of loam, the bones of trees,
   Rocks the size of skulls.
To see these secrets of the soil
   Feels vaguely terrible.

A landmark's gone. I grieve it.
   The pine earned local fame,
A claim on our affection,
   And then the big wind came.

Those of us who pass this way
   Will feel that something's wrong,
Though hungry saplings pushing up
   Say: Not for long.

Solo

I woke from a dream about my first wife
To the tick-tick of leaves drifting down on the tent.
All these past lives! I saw stars
Spread like spawn in a still, black pond
And lay awake a long time, recalling old lovers,
Listening to wind strip leaves off the trees,
The cat-scream of one limb rubbing another.

I never thought I'd ever see
A fox go scamper up a tree
And there, pissed off and weasel-mean,
Create a ruckus, make a scene,
Glower, growl so frightfully
You'd think he thought that, rightfully,
My grub belonged to him, not me.
Well, he's got spunk, that's plain to see.
I grin and raise my mug of tea.

A Short Story About Loons

We paddled out that morning
And smiled at three loons,
A mother and her puffballs.
I muttered, "Oh, for cute."
They followed close behind her;
She called them with soft hoots.

Returning by the same route,
We saw she couldn't find her
Small ones anywhere. "Oh, shoot,"
You said. Her frantic calls
Destroyed the afternoon,
Which echoed with her mourning.

The Otters

God knows, we would have been content with golden fish
That day, but the silver river overflowed with gifts.
As we held our glinting walleyes high to gloat and cheer,
A chuckling clan of otters suddenly appeared.
We hadn't seen their submarine approach. They just were there
And interested, exchanging our excited stares,
Submerging, bobbing up right close beside the boat
To gawk and peer. These living, breathing periscopes
Were talkative; they chattered, gurgled, hissed, and chirred
So that we whispered first, then laughed at what we heard.
Their playfulness and whiskers called up cats,
But the otters didn't mind their fur was running wet.
Some looked alert, concerned, but others just as glad
As children in some happy past that none of us had had.
Their beach ball buoyancy reminded us of seals.
Like seals, they seemed related, made us feel
As if these river silkies could easily turn human,
Slip their fur, emerge as little men and women.
Like us, they love their watersports. We saw them dive
To loop the loop, backfloat, flipflop, dunk, and rise.
Their posh pelts glistened, their pelage silver-gray
As the river and the rippling overcast that day
I saw that happiness was possible on earth,
At least in water, and what I witnessed gradually gave birth
To the dream that once upon a time we all were otters
And performed erotic undulations underwater.

Dead Gull

Did you fly too near the sun?
You look both burnt and drowned—
You, who transformed trash and stinking fish
To graceful flight, whose bones were light,
Whose cries were bright in the twinkling air.
You never wondered what you were
But coupled quickly with your kind,
Gobbled your food ecstatically,
Screamed at the world self-righteously,
Swooped and veered, climbed and hung
Splayed in the sky like a star. How far
You have fallen. The feathers of your carcass stir,
But you will not rise again. The autumn wind
Tears at my hair and makes a terrific noise.
God is a dog, and we are stuffed toys.

Chickadee

Like seedy stuff?
Can't get enough?
Ball of fluff
Seeks little puff.
Big appetite
But sleek and light.
Cute black cap
And black cravat,
White underthroat,
Gray overcoat.
Picks at bits
And likes to flit
Nice and quick
From stick to stick.
Would know your song
In any throng,
Those special notes
From your soft throat,
As sharp and sweet
As thistle seed.
Skills to weave
You won't believe.
Can build the nest
To your request.
Not too fussy.
Always busy.
Will not brood.
Will sing for food,
Go to and fro
At ten below.
Still will trill
When all is chill.
Downy soft
With lots of loft.

Like what you see?
Then check out me,
Chick chickadee,
Me, me, me, me,
Me, me, me, me!

Driving the high bridge over the bay,
I saw an eagle, real and regal,
Sailing at my side. Delighted,
Elated, for one full minute
I was a World War I fighter pilot
Steering my triplane through the wreckage
Of the heavens, cheered by my comrade, my chum,
Who protected my off-wing until he peeled away
And I descended to the distant, ordinary shore.

And then there was the wolf, my first,
For which I'd waited fifty years,
Listening with my skin, watching with my hair,
Whenever I ranged the woods,
Where I heard rumors, picked up scat.
But he showed up unpredictably,
Forty feet off the interstate, romping in the ditch,
An overgrown dog with heavy head,
Grizzled bronze and gold, gold-eyed,
And I was gone, whisked along in traffic,
Pounding on the steering wheel and shouting,
"Wolf! A wolf! Son of a bitch!"

Not to mention that early summer moose,
Knee-deep in the bog at the bend of the road.
My brother hollered, "Whoa!"
And I obeyed, stopped cold,
Though we could have been hit from behind.
His coat was rough and scruffy,
Gunnysacks smeared with grease,
But he was a moose, all right, a mountain
Of flesh and fat, enough to feed a family
Well on through the winter. He looked
Rank and gamy, tough and dangerous,

Masculine to the core: wet beard, big prick,
A velvet crown of antlers he carried like a king.
What were we to make of such a living thing?

Or any of those many other sudden offerings?
The doe in her bright-red summer coat,
The raggedy vixen with her kit, dumb cluck
Spruce grouse, partridge off like a shot,
Scurry of squirrel, rabbity flash,
The great gray owl turning its face
Like a satellite dish, wink of weasel,
Slink of mink, the ass end of a bear?
Or that cougar I saw through veils of snow
Years ago on the Gunflint Trail,
The lash of its tawny tail.

We smashed through ancient kingdoms,
Ramming our wide highways home,
Rivers of concrete, tar, and gravel.
The animals had no choice. Nervous, edgy,
Exposed, they flushed along the margins.
Each creature, though, seemed a gift,
A luminescent moment that opened, froze the mind,
Before it melted. Always, I felt chilled, thrilled,
Washed and warmed with gladness, blessed.

But what did they mean to say,
Those animals glimpsed from the road? Nothing
Human at all? Or simply, "Hey!" "Hi!" "How do you do?"
I'd call those encounters accidents only,
Only darker thoughts are forming
In clouds at the back of my skull,
Thoughts that can't get through,
In a language I can't recall—shrieks,
Hoots, barks, growls, an agonizing howl—
Alarming, something sinister . . . a warning.

Black Bear Among Blueberries

for Dex Thue

At first he seemed a patch of dirt,
    But then we saw him move.
We paddled till our triceps hurt;
    He grew and slowly proved
A creeping bear, preoccupied
With fruit like fallen bits of sky.

My buddy's camera chirred and clicked.
    I steadied the canoe,
And then, to get a better look,
    He shouted, "Hey! Hey, you!"
The brute knew English well enough
To stand up straight and stare at us.

The bear looked like a patch of dirt
    In snaps the photo shop
Sent back. That burly, earthy spirit
    Had somehow slipped our trap.
The zoom had failed, or we had not
Been half as close as we had thought.

No evidence would help us brag
    About what we had seen,
His bulk and weight, his bristly shag
    So black it had a sheen,
Or how he rose, as tall as us,
To show that he could maul us.

He turned and ambled up the hill,
    Stepped through a wall of trees,
And though we knew they seldom kill
    Our kind, we walked uneasily

Across that hillside berry patch
And kept an eye out, naturally.

The place had been attacked, ransacked,
   Deadfalls overturned
For grubs, the boulders tilted back
   For beetles and sweet worms.
We crouched and filled our hats with fruit,
Though he had left few shrubs to loot.

Those berries taste like wind and sky.
   The hunger of that bear
Was not unlike our appetite,
   So why should we be scared?
It hardly seemed the jaws of death
Would exhale sweet blueberry breath.

And yet we eyed the ridgeline
   Where he had disappeared
Among the shadows of the jack pines
   And felt a twinge of fear.
This world was still a wilderness
Deserving awe and watchfulness.

Yellow Waterlilies on the Langley River

I slip and slither down the grassy riverbank,
Practically cartwheel and crash in the stream,
Recover and launch my peapod boat,
Slide beneath the small cement bridge,
And paddle black water for a short quarter mile,
Half dizzy, bedazzled by midsummer sun.

Now I turn, having seen more than enough
To know I'll be back on a lazier day.
The canoe comes about, and I hear myself shout,
"Where in the hell is Claude Monet?"

The bridge is gilded, the water glows,
Lilies lift their blossoms
Like small, gold balls, the raised fists
Of infants rejoicing in heaven.
Rejoicing, I join them, Moses
In the bulrushes for fifteen minutes,
And Pharaoh's men are far away.
If I waken, let me waken
To flowers and women.
The canoe is a coffin.
I'm crossing over.
Rock me. Rock me.
Rockabye, baby.

The lilies have leaves the size of saucers,
Scattered on the stream like green valentines.
I want to say, "I love you, too."
But there's nobody here
But black spruce, gold lilies,
The winking, blinking, glittering air.

Little Caesar

Lefty Larsen, an epileptic
Vietnam vet, fell crazy in love
With canoe country, went off downriver
And up the creek, with a paddle, fish pole,
An overstuffed pack, and nobody knew
If he'd ever come back.
      After the war,
He found the country he was fighting for;
The citizens were ravens, eagles, and loons,
The air perfume of pine and spruce.
In the holy hush of his own company,
On a granite slab, in the jack-pine shade,
Lefty made a kind of personal truce.

Bought a small place up in Beaver Bay,
Where the locals dubbed him Little Caesar
In honor of his frequent seizures.
Paperwork betrayed him. He was on meds.
The state took his driver's license away,
But Lefty didn't give a flying fuck.
Neither did the sheriff or the state patrol.
Everybody knew his rusted-out truck,
Topped with a fleet of battered canoes.
When Lefty felt his mouth go dry,
He'd pull to the shoulder or drive
In the ditch, stretch and kick
Till his fit was over. He'd lie there
And twitch while the cars banged by.
It wasn't like somebody was going to die.

Good with kids, he taught them how to fish,
Enchanting them with non-stop chatter:
"He's suckin' your leech. Set the hook!
Tip up. Tip up! You got him. No!
Son, you just let a trophy go."

You could say Lefty had a case of the bends
From the way he rode that riverflow.
He got to know all the walleye holes
And stashed his gear at his favorite sites,
As if that river belonged to him,
Built bonfires to drive back the night
And watched the sparks climb out of sight.
Some folks worried he'd come to harm,
But Lefty went twenty-seven days one time
And only lost the skin off both his arms
From too much bug dope, maximum Deet.

The water was wide. The water was sweet.
Lefty's friends all knew he'd drown.
They'd seen him drop in his canoe,
Shudder and buck, shake and flail
Like a fresh-caught fish in a metal pail.
But Lefty had scored an airline jacket:
"If a fit comes on, and I fall out,
I yank this cord. The thing inflates.
No sweat, man. I'm sure to float."
Lefty was tough. He could hack it.
And the little bastard never went down.

But Lefty had problems. His brain seized up.
He turned into a drooling babbler.
He's living with his brother down South somewhere,
But we still talk about him up around here.
Lefty wasn't bland, like me and you.
Lefty had character. He was one, too.

Lefty, come out, wherever you are.
The Milky Way is a river of stars.

How will you get from here to there?
How on earth will you find the way?
Read the horizon. Look sharp. See
How the raggedy treeline sinks?
The portage is probably back in a bay.
Would you choose to hump over a hill
With packs or a boat on your back?
Look for the lows, a notch or a sag
That very well might be the place
Where a wiggling creek seeps in
Or lakewater leaks away.
With luck, you'll detect a blaze
Head-high on a shoreline tree,
A scar the size of your hand,
Where somebody long before you
Whacked off bark with an axe.
Say thanks. You've been given a sign,
A guide that could save your life
To lose on another day. Pull in
And watch out. This is a place
Where you might dump. Extract
The packs from the boat and rest
That fat one there in the shade.
The small one goes on your back.

Now you may flatten your palm
Against the smooth of the blaze.
This laying on of the hand
Reverses the faith healer's art,
For wood is good, as you know,
And energy flows up your arm.
You might want to freshen the wound,
Scraping it raw with a knife
To signal some other lost soul,

But likely you'd just as soon
The forest grew shut at your back.
So let it stay, silvery gray
As the sky on a cloudy day.

Now shoulder the narrow canoe
And vanish into the woods.
No telling what lies ahead—
You may wallow in goop to your thighs,
Bumble through boulders and stones,
Or creep up a slippery cliff.
If the trail is a comfortable rut,
You can put your faith in your feet
And those who have gone before,
But you've probably chosen a path
To take you out back of beyond,
Where you'll have to step over the dead
Trees in your way and big rocks
That call for hopscotch ballet.
You'll dance with the boat on your head
And just about now might recall
How the Buddha told us no man,
Having crossed the water to shore,
Would hoist the raft on his head
And bear it away overland.
Never mind. Have a laugh.
Say you went to a different school
Or confess that you're Buddha's fool.
At least if the sky drops rain,
You'll have a roof over your head.
But you can't live here. Push on.
If the path peters out at your feet,
Disappears in a heap of dry leaves,
You'll have to reverse, retreat
And search the trunks for a blaze,
A match for that sign on the shore,
To show you the way for sure.

Now, as you head uphill,
Still wearing your very long hat,
Your brow and chin both drip,
Your breath escapes in a hiss,
And you enter the world of myth.
You feel for your brother, Sisyphus,
And, reaching the ridgeline, revolt,
Easing the nose of the boat
Into the crotch of a birch,
And step out from under the weight.
Blood pumps into your neck;
The ache oozes out of your back.
You can breathe the peppermint air
And shake the bugs out of your hair.

You must take up your burden again,
Your arms upraised, outstretched,
As if you were falling headlong
Or shouting perpetual praise.
And now as you suffer uphill,
You utter the name of Christ.
You, too, have been scourged and lashed,
If only by branches and weeds.
You, too, have been torn by thorns,
But the blood that tickles your face
Has only been drawn by flies,
Who scribble their meaningless drivel
Inches before your eyes.
This dead-leg limping uphill
Is good for the heart but hard.
You can tell your body who's boss,
But every thirty-odd yards
The blazes slowly rise
Like stations of the cross.

You're glad for gravity now,
Pulling you thumping downhill,
Glad for that yellow swallowtail
Splayed on a balsam bough,

Glad for the magic of moss
And the deer mouse crossing the trail,
And though your breathing is wheezing now,
Your heart loud in your head,
Your mind stays cool and notices
Those blazes all are faces
Of the dead who rescued you:
That teacher who admonished you,
The uncle who took you to lunch,
That aunt who called you "dear" and "doll,"
Your dad, who ran beside your bike
And slowly let you go,
Your mother dreaming and smoothing the swell
Of her belly before you were born.

The dead go by in a blur,
And, gasping, faster, faster now,
You flash past the last blaze
And stumble on down to trail's end,
Teeter and rock, and now, dear God,
Push up, over, and drop
The impossibly heavy prow
In the buoyant blue water below.

You may feel you've finally arrived,
But once your hot head has cooled,
You'll remember, Buddha's fool,
You have to go back for that pack.
Walk, for the night is coming
Up over the edge of the earth,
And you shouldn't get caught in the dark,
Or you'll find yourself lost back there,
Embracing all the wrong trees,
Fingers groping rough bark,
Feeling for that smooth blaze
Like a blind man reading a face.

Stony River

I am trying to remember
That blue bend in the river,
The pines and yellow grasses.
How quickly my life passes.

The air out there was incense,
Essence of September.
Was it peppermint and anise?
I really can't remember.

I am trying to remember
The way the water glittered,
Sunlight like a benediction,
But that afternoon is gone.

I am trying to remember
Those minnows bright as embers,
How like sparks they flashed and vanished
In the pool below the rapids.

I heard a bird or two, as I remember,
The splashing of my paddle in the river,
The trickle when I lifted it, and then there were
Those rumors in the breeze that made me shiver.

I am trying to remember
That eagle soaring over
And the shorebirds by the stones,
But those creatures all have flown.

Every autumn now I tell myself: Remember
To get out there on the river
Under golden leaves that cling to crooked branches.
We only get so many chances.

That daytrip through the jack pines and the willows
Is fading like the music of a cello.
Nothing in this life will last forever,
Though I hoped it might while floating down the river.

The Underword

As I knelt to clean the bass I'd caught,
I heard a sound a man might make
If he'd been slugged by a heavyweight,
The primitive expletive "Unh!"
I grunted back, got a rude response,
So I walked to the lake to look.
A big bull moose stood across the way,
Up to his knees in the bay.
His hide looked smooth and shiny black;
His rack was fresh and huge.
He splashed along the distant shore,
Calling repeatedly: "Unh!"
What could he want? It couldn't be food.
There were lilies and sedges galore.
He was looking for love or a fight.
That groan recalled the guts of thought,
The sound beneath all speech,
A word from the land of Ur.
It was laden with pain, desire, and pride.
It said what I felt when my parents died,
When I first caught sight of my wife.
This was the poem I'd been longing for,
True as the blade of a knife,
The original syllable "Unh!"
I watched that bull march into the west,
Thrashing the silver water white,
Calling incessantly as he went,
As if he carried a wound.
Late September. The air grown cold.
I saw what the moose couldn't know:
As he waded into the dying light,
His antlers had turned to gold.

Pike Lake Lullaby

for Lilo

Clouds in the water,
Clouds in the sky.
Trees on the shoreline
Shine in the lake.
Am I dreaming I'm dreaming
Or finally awake?
My father is fading.
My mother is dirt.
I can't remember anything
About my birth.
So how did I get here?
I happened along.
The wind in the white pines
Sounds like a song
Saying, Hush now. Quiet.
Nothing is wrong.

Acknowledgments

I am grateful to the editors of the following magazines in which some of these poems, or earlier versions of them, first appeared:

North Coast Review: "Flying the Flag," "Not Sleeping at Bill Holm's House," "The Rusty Wheelbarrow," "This," "The Thousand-foot Ore Boat";

North Dakota Quarterly: "Sober Song," "Sunday Morning";

NorthLife: "Fall Flowers";

Poetry: "Night Fishing, Lake Polly";

Reader Weekly: "Dick Cheney's Heart," "The Liberal Media," "The Neocon Con," "The President's Prayer";

South Dakota Review: "Anniversary";

Southern Humanities Review: "The Underword";

Spirituality & Health: "Block Party," "Icebreaker," "The Old Corral";

Tar River Poetry: "Black Bear Among Blueberries," "A Circle of Rock," "Mrs. Winters";

Wisconsin Academy Review: "Dorothea," "Sunflowers";

Wolfhead Quarterly: "Before Supper";

Your Life: "The Necklace," "Yardwork."

"Another Country" and "At Quaker Meeting" are reprinted with permission from the March 2004 issue of *Chronicles: A Magazine of American Culture*, a publication of The Rockford Institute in Rockford, Illinois.

"Peregrine" first appeared in the anthology *Urban Nature* edited by Laure-Anne Bosselaar and published by Milkweed Editions in 2000.

Two Individual Artist Fellowships from the Arrowhead Regional Arts Council, a Travel & Study Grant from the Jerome Foundation, and a Faculty/Staff Stipend from the University of Wisconsin, Superior, allowed me to complete some of these poems.

Thanks to my wife, Dorothea Diver, and to my stepdaughters, Lilo and Bettina Stuecher, for their criticism, patience, and faith.

Thanks to Anthony Bukoski, Philip Dacey, Milan Kovacovic, Ellie Schoenfeld, and Connie Wanek, whose comments helped me improve this book.

Thanks to Steve Huff, Thom Ward, and all hands at BOA Editions for their thoughtful work on this collection.

About the Author

Barton Sutter is the only author to win the Minnesota Book Award in three different categories: for fiction with *My Father's War and Other Stories*, for creative nonfiction with *Cold Comfort: Life at the Top of the Map*, and for poetry with *The Book of Names: New and Selected Poems*. Among other honors, he has won a Jerome Foundation Travel & Study Grant (Sweden), a Loft-McKnight Award, and the Bassine Citation from the Academy of American Poets. He has adapted his poems for the stage, written for public radio, and performs as one half of The Sutter Brothers, a poetry-and-music duo. For more than three decades, he has explored the canoe country along the Canadian border. A resident of Duluth since 1987, he teaches at the University of Wisconsin, Superior.

.

BOA EDITIONS, LTD.

AMERICAN POETS CONTINUUM SERIES

No. 1 *The Fuhrer Bunker: A Cycle of Poems in Progress*
W. D. Snodgrass

No. 2 *She*
M. L. Rosenthal

No. 3 *Living With Distance*
Ralph J. Mills, Jr.

No. 4 *Not Just Any Death*
Michael Waters

No. 5 *That Was Then: New and Selected Poems*
Isabella Gardner

No. 6 *Things That Happen Where There Aren't Any People*
William Stafford

No. 7 *The Bridge of Change: Poems 1974–1980*
John Logan

No. 8 *Signatures*
Joseph Stroud

No. 9 *People Live Here: Selected Poems 1949–1983*
Louis Simpson

No. 10 *Yin*
Carolyn Kizer

No. 11 *Duhamel: Ideas of Order in Little Canada*
Bill Tremblay

No. 12 *Seeing It Was So*
Anthony Piccione

No. 13 *Hyam Plutzik: The Collected Poems*

No. 14 *Good Woman: Poems and a Memoir 1969–1980*
Lucille Clifton

No. 15 *Next: New Poems*
Lucille Clifton

No. 16 *Roxa: Voices of the Culver Family*
William B. Patrick

No. 17 *John Logan: The Collected Poems*

No. 18 *Isabella Gardner: The Collected Poems*

No. 19 *The Sunken Lightship*
Peter Makuck

No. 20 *The City in Which I Love You*
Li-Young Lee

No. 21 *Quilting: Poems 1987–1990*
Lucille Clifton

No. 22 *John Logan: The Collected Fiction*

No. 23 *Shenandoah and Other Verse Plays*
Delmore Schwartz

No. 24 *Nobody Lives on Arthur Godfrey Boulevard*
Gerald Costanzo

No. 25 *The Book of Names: New and Selected Poems*
Barton Sutter

No. 26 *Each in His Season*
W. D. Snodgrass

No. 27 *Wordworks: Poems Selected and New*
Richard Kostelanetz

No. 28 *What We Carry*
Dorianne Laux

No. 29 *Red Suitcase*
Naomi Shihab Nye

No. 30 *Song*
Brigit Pegeen Kelly

No. 31 *The Fuehrer Bunker: The Complete Cycle*
W. D. Snodgrass

No. 32 *For the Kingdom*
Anthony Piccione

No. 33 *The Quicken Tree*
Bill Knott

No. 34 *These Upraised Hands*
William B. Patrick

No. 35 *Crazy Horse in Stillness*
William Heyen

No. 36 *Quick, Now, Always*
Mark Irwin

Colophon

Farewell to the Starlight in Whiskey, Poems by Barton Sutter,
was set in Goudy by Richard Foerster, York Beach, Maine.
The cover design is by Ben Peterson.
The cover photograph, "The Back of Bart's Head" by Dexter Thue,
is courtesy of the photographer.
Manufacturing was by United Graphics, Inc., Mattoon, Illinois.

The publication of this book was made possible in part by the special
support of the following individuals:

Mary & Arthur Aufderheide
Alan & Nancy Cameros ❋ Burch & Louise Craig
Bradley P. & Debra Kang Dean
Suzanne & Peter Durant
Kathleen P. Ford
Dr. Henry & Beverly French
Gerard & Suzanne Gouvernet ❋ Judy & Dane Gordon
Kip & Deb Hale
Peter & Robin Hursh
Robert & Willy Hursh
Archie & Pat Kutz
Patty & David Leach ❋ James P. Lenfestey
Rosemary & Lew Lloyd
Peter & Phyllis Makuck
Jeffrey Marks
Peter Oddleifson & Kay Wallace ❋ Boo Poulin
Deborah Ronnen
Bruce & Madeleine Sweet
Robert & Lee Ward ❋ Thomas R. Ward
Pat & Michael Wilder
Glenn & Helen William ❋ C. S. Wilson
Deb & Edith Wylder

❋